Thrifty Prepping

Tips How To Be a Smart Prepper

And Spend Less

Table of Contents

Introduction: Some Initial Preps

No matter what happens, you've got to be prepared. Those are words to live by. You used to know a guy that was such an obsessed prepper that he spent nearly a million dollars on prep supplies. But what if you've got to stretch that dollar just a little bit further? Don't worry.

This book goes through some of the best ways to get the most from the least amount of money. Because in the economic uncertainty of today, sometimes it's all we can do to have enough money to buy groceries let alone an elaborate solar panel system. This book will help you stretch that dollar a whole heck of a lot farther!

Chapter 1: Gaining Your Own Power

Millions of people today are depending on an aging infrastructure that has been euphemistically called the "Grid". This aging, and near obsolete power network is due for a tune up to say the least, and the often inept and inefficient workings it espouses is simply a recipe for disaster. This has led many to seek alternatives to this grid based energy. Many ideas have been proposed in order to escape this energy bottleneck.

Several people for example, have strived to take their energy needs into their own hands by strapping solar panels onto the roof of their home. But while solar power is a great way to collect energy, the standard solar power setup can become quite expensive. In order to buy and install a conventional solar panel system you could end up spending upwards of $5000 or more. Most of us just don't have that much money to fork of on just a whim. So what are some cheaper methods of saving or even gaining free energy? Read this chapter to find out more!

Replace Light Bulbs

One of the easiest things that you could ever do when it comes to saving energy in your home is to simply replace your light bulbs, especially when it comes to light bulbs that emit light for more than one hour a day. Thee light bulbs have what is known as a light emitting diode. I have found numerous occasions in which I have switched from regular bulbs to fluorescent and have been able to save a tremendous amount of money.

Insulate Your Windows

This is an even simpler yet cost effective way in which you could save some money in your home. Closing the shades is a simple way that you can keep your heat *inside* your home during the summer and also keep warmth *in* during the winter. It is an easy thing that anyone can do, but it is also very cost effective in the long run. It has been scientifically proven that a good set of drapes can cut heat depreciation in half.

Just be sure to have your drapes hanging loose, so that they don't block heat vents and air ducts. You should most especially close the drapes that you have on your north facing windows in order to make sure that the chilly air you have is kept out during the winter time, one of the best ways that you can insulate your window however is to use plastic and vinyl sheeting and attach it to the interior of your windows. In order to attach this plastic to your windows you should take some weatherproofed tape and use it to hold that plastic in place.

Use Moderation with Your Thermostat

Keep your thermostat set to 68 degrees in the winter time and set to 78 degrees during the summer. With just this little bit of moderation you can make sure that you keep your bill as low as possible. Many people overdo their AC in the summer and along with raising their bill they cause their AC units to prematurely expire!

You have a similar problem during the winter as well, because for many of us during the winter time, when we wake up during a particularly cold morning, or when we first come in from the cold we are tempted to crank the heat up as much as possible! But then by the time the thermostat reaches 75 degrees, only then do we realize that we have overdone it! So in that sense, it is always the best policy to keep your thermostat in the moderate range of 68 degrees during the winter, and no more than 78 degrees during the summer.

Using Slightly Damaged Solar Cells

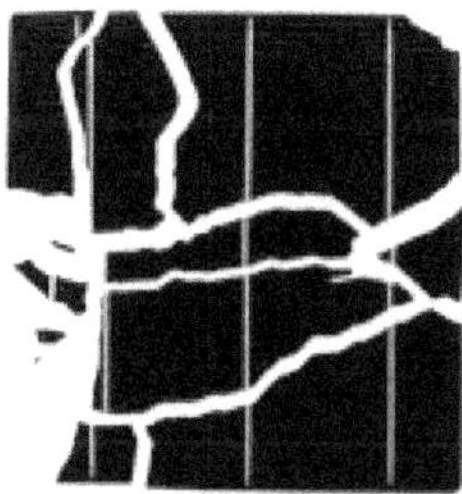

Even though you can pay a pretty penny for a fully functional solar panel, you will find that you can save a lot of money when it comes to buying slightly damaged solar cells. These cells can be taken and placed in a wooden frame and made into a fully functioning self built solar apparatus.

You can usually find these slightly damaged solar cells at online retailers such as Amazon and EBay. These solar cells may have chips or scratches in them, cosmetically marring their surface, but they are still more than able to collect the solar energy you would need to power your home and pinch those pennies.

Wind Power

Just like the sun, wind is another source of renewable energy that can be scooped up and used just about anywhere. Most of these wind makers that are on the market today consist of a horizontally oriented axis which utilizes "upwind" from the device, by extending three fiberglass blades forward. These blades are known as the "swept area", since it is the part of the assembly that manages to sweep in the most wind that it can, while the tail keeps the whole structure balanced.

Use the Power Pot

The Power Pot is a great new addition to the world of cheap energy, because this one makes the process of charging all of your electronics completely free as long as you have your Power Pot with you. The Power Pot works by utilizing hot water particles when they are heated and then transferring that energy directly through USB ports. Once heated, you can use this to then charge your laptop, phone, and other devices.

Conserve Energy form your Fridge

This may seem like a more mundane penny pincher, but it can certainly save you a lot of money. Because the simple fact remains, the refrigerator can cost you more energy than any other part of your home. In order to avoid losing energy from this appliance you need to only open your fridge when necessary. Some of the biggest wasters of energy, believe it or not, are the people who stand around with a fridge door open for no apparent reason.

Don't just open the fridge because you are bored and want to count your tomatoes! Simply open the fridge when you really need to! Another way that cold air can leave a refrigerator is for air to escape the seal of the door. Make sure that the seal is always tight, and if not take the time to replace it. Along with these energy saving measures, perhaps the best thing you can do, is to adjust the thermostat inside, and move it up from the typical 32 degrees to 42 degrees. Your food will still be able to be kept cold at this temperature, and you will save a lot of extra money!

Give Your Water Heater a Boost

People don't realize it, but they can expend a lot of energy through frivolous use of hot water. In fact, as much as 19 percent of your utility bill can be attributed to how your water heater is being used when it comes to your hot water. In order to save money on your energy bill, the first thing that you need to do is to do stop taking baths!

No, that doesn't mean you have to be dirty and scrounge the rest of your life! No we don't mean don't *bathe* we're just saying don't take a *bath*. Believe it or not, taking a shower can save on your water heating expense, much more than a bath ever could. So when you can, always try to opt for a good old shower rather than an energy consuming bath. Another great tip for reducing the cost of your water heater is to install a low-flow aerator that can limit the amount of water that can come out of your shower head.

Conserve Your Car's Fuel

The first thing that you can do in order to improve your car's gas mileage is to avoid idling your car as much as possible. Idling the car just burns up precious fuel while not actually taking you anywhere, avoid doing this. And despite what you may have heard, even on the coldest winter days you really don't need to "warm up" your car, any more than about 30 seconds before you take off. Driving the car warms it up much better, and faster than just sitting in place with the engine running.

Otherwise you are just burning through your fuel supply and needlessly polluting the air! Another way to get god gas mileage is to abstain from reckless driving that causes you to rapidly accelerate, speed, or slam on your brakes. All of these activities can lower your gas mileage as much as 33%. Speed is a factor that can not be discounted either. Just think about it, when you are going 60 miles per hour, every 5 miles you travel at that rate of speed you are burning through about 35 cents of gasoline! So just play it cool on your accelerator so you can avoid sticker shock at the pump!

Chapter 2: Cheap Ways to Grow and Stock Food for Disaster!

Food prices are going up every single day. In order to combat these rises in inflation, one of the best things that you could do would be to devise a way in which you would not have to be at the mercy of the grocery and his stickers. The easiest way to do some this is to grow, store and stock your own food all year round. In this chapter we will explore how you can o just that.

Backyard Garden

Anyone with a just a little bit of room in their backyard can have a backyard garden. To create one you just need to determine where your garden bed and pathways are going to be. The garden path is crucial because it will determine where you can walk to water your plants without stepping on them. Always be aware of this layout before you begin. The backyard garden bed's dimensions should generally be about 2 feet in width and 10 feet in length.

This will provide you with the best kind of set up for the space that you have and the amount of water that you are going to use. To get started put what is known as a "digging board" down into the earth right where your garden bed is going to be. It is from here that you will begin digging your first garden bed. Dig about 1 foot deep, 4 feet wide, and 10 feet in length. Now take all of the dirt that you have dug out and save it in a bucket or some other container for later use.

Once your first garden bed has been dug out, move your board over right next to the head of this first bed and start digging all over again using the same formula and dimensions of 1 foot deep, 4 feet wide, and 10 feet long. Repeat this process as many times as you like. Once all of your beds have been dug out, go to your bucket and sprinkle about 1 inch of that freshly dug soil over each one of your beds.

With the remaining soil in your soil you can then create a compost type mixture. Do this by gathering up some broken plant material such as leaves and sticks, break them up and put them down in the bucket of dirt. Stir this compacted material together in the bucket.

Now put down about an inch of this compost soil down in each of your garden beds. Let this sit for about a day, and after that you can begin planting. Just plant your seeds as you would in any other soil. Dig about 3 inches deep, pack down the dirt and make sure that the plants are separated evenly between each other. Just water these plants and watch them grow!

Raise Urban Livestock

In recent years the self sufficient phenomenon known as "Urban Homesteading" has really took off. And among the most popular and enriching things that can be done as an Urban Homesteader is to raise your own livestock. This may at first seem like a daunting task within city limits but if it is done right it is fully achievable.

If you would like to do this however, the first thing that you need to do is check with your local city governance to get an understanding of what animals you are allowed to have on your property in your area. Most urban areas nowadays have at least a small allowance for a few chickens and rabbits so this would be a great place to begin. For these livestock creatures you can make a chicken coop and a rabbit hutch in order to hold them.

The structures for these habitats are very similar, they basically consist of a large wooden box with wire mesh flooring that allows the animals to defecate, and have their droppings fall down onto the ground below them. Chickens are great, fairly low maintenance animals, and they can be fed on just about anything. These hardy little critters have been known to survive on just scraps. Rabbits on the other hand will most likely need healthy multi-vitamin pellets in order to be at their best.

These rabbit pellets can be found at most pet stores. Once our chicken and rabbits are in good health you can then either market them or keep them around for your own use. Chickens in particular are a great way to beat the sticker shock at the grocer, since they will enable you to have fresh eggs year round. You can of course butcher the chickens for their meat as well, and the same goes for the rabbits. Besides meat the only other purpose of raising rabbits would be to sell them. And there is quite a bit of money that can be made there as well.

Utilize a Root Cellar

Cellars have been around for a long time, and their good use when it come to preserving food have never really went out of style. A cellar is simply any structure that goes underground and utilizes the coolness of the earth to keep food cold. Many old houses used to have root cellars attached just outside of their homes, but even if you don't have a root cellar in the classic sense you could always take a basement and convert it into one.

This is done by just walling off one of the corners of the basement with some plywood. Just make sure that there is a window close by so that you can have ventilation and this walled off corner can preserve your food while pinching your pennies with the energy that you save with this all natural cooling system.

Build a Mini Greenhouse

A greenhouse will enable you to greatly cut the cost of your grocery bill by allowing you to grow your veggies year round. But alas, not all of us have the resources to be able to grow plants in a standard greenhouse. But that's okay, because we can create our own mini greenhouse that won't take up any space at all. All you really need to do this one is some 2x4's, some plastic and tape.

Just take four wooden 2x4's and place them in a square formation over a free area of land, this serve as the walls of your green house. Once this frame is in place you can the plant your seeds right there inside the borders of the frame. Now just place your plastic over the frame and using strong tape, secure the plastic to the sides of the frame. Now you have a covered, protected area in which your plants can stay warm and absorb as much directed sunlight as possible in order to ensure the best growth.

Produce Dried Meat

With this penny pinching DIY you can make your own jerky that can last you for the whole year. To get started you will need to create a salty brine solution in which you can soak your meat. Your brine should consist of one pound of salt per each gallon of water. Once your meat has been thoroughly brined in this solution you can then stretch them out on some ventilated meat trays and allow them to dry out in the sun. Soon these strips of meat will be dried out and you will have some great jerky to munch on in the months ahead.

Do Your Own Canning

Canning isn't hard. In order to can your own food all you need is a canning jar and a way to heat the contents of that jar up enough hat the jar will develop an airtight seal. The lid for your canning jar is a screw band that goes on top of a metal top. Screw this tight and then place your jar inside a large metal pot, fill it with water and boil the contents on high heat.

Boil your jar at these levels for at least 5 minutes, afterward the seal should have formed and your jar will be canned. Now just let the jar cool down before putting it away for storage. When you are a real pinch and food prices are going up, all of the penny pinching strategies presented in this chapter can really carry you the extra mile.

Chapter 3: Penny Pinching Your Communication

Our cell phone bills and internet charges sometimes make our mouth drop to the floor when we hear about them. In this chapter we will focus on how you can reduce or even eliminate much of this cot as you learn to penny punch your communication bill!

Use Ham Radio

Since the advent of Ham Radio, people have been hamming up the airways for over a century. This mode of communication is not only free; it's a whole lot of fun! Ham radio does not depend on the grid or any other kind of infrastructure. Ham Radio depends on a simple network of fellow enthusiasts that boost their signal as they operate together. Once your ham rig is established the airwaves you operate on are totally free. So that way even if disaster strikes and you can't even afford to pay your cell phone bill, you will be able to still get a message across on the radio.

Install ISP Search

If you area struggling under the oppressive regime of an ISP dictatorship that is sucking all of your money out of your bank account then you just might want to install an ISP search. Installing this app will allow you to punch in your zip code and then pull up a browser with a listing of all possible ISP's in your area. By asking around from this list you could end up saving a lot of money on your internet connection. I saved quite a bundle the first time that I tried it myself.

Use Public Wi-Fi

If you have a penchant for the latest movie releases, songs, and other multimedia, yet you are in some serious need of penny pinching, one of the best things for you to do is to use public Wi-Fi in order to fulfill them. Many common public places such as McDonalds and Starbucks have free Wi-Fi that is open to the public. At these places you can easily enjoy a hamburger or cappuccino while you download a 2 hour movie. You can then watch the movie later at your leisure later on. It sure beats having to pay for a streaming service. So be wise, pinch those pennies and start saving that money!

Use Land Line Phones

For many they are an extreme vestige from the past, but land line phones can be used today just as well as they could be used yesterday, and they are not dependent on cell phone towers that are often unreliable. All you have to do in order to get your landline phone installed is call up a conventional phone company and have them put the line into your home. You can also benefit from the use of VOIP, and use it for the shockingly low price of $9.95 a month; these are all great ways to save a lot of money on your monthly communication expenses.

Data Cap

These data cap's are notorious for their use as ways in which the ISP provider can take more money out of the pocket of the consumer. Comcast in particular is notorious for this, typically enforcing a data cap at about 300 GB a month. These users are then charge about $10 more every single month under this regimen. If you find yourself in this kind of predicament and you need to save money, then the best thing that you should do is go off and find another provider without such limitations as soon as possible. Yes my friends, if you wish to save money on your communication bill you should most definitely get rid of that data cap.

Communicate Through CB Radio

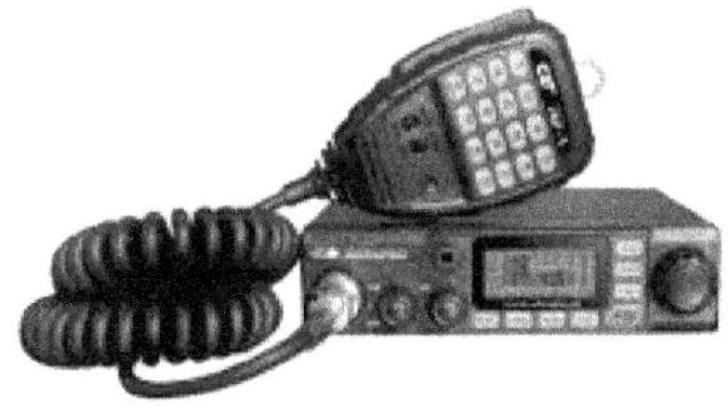

CB radio serves as a classic communication alternative, it's known as the main form of communication for the truck driver, but it can be known for a whole lot more. The CB in CB radio stands for citizens band radio and it is called this for a reason, because it is for all the citizens of the world that this radio station is created. CB has been around the block for a little bit, first originating in the early 1960's.

But since that time it has been utilized by police fire and all other emergency personnel. CB typically runs on 27 MHz band width and it works as a two way communication channel and works by giving the other person a "handle". The "handle" is the means by which you can communicate with others. If the cell phone towers go down and if everything else falls through the cracks, you will then be able to still speak through CB radio. CB communication is a great way to get out the word when you have no other way to communicate.

Use a Hand Cranked Radio

These things are a true marvel and they work well as emergency radios. All you have to do is use a little elbow grease and crank those baby's up so that your radio stations will come to life. While you won't be able to send any messages out to through this radio you will be able to listen to important radio stations on AM and FM so that you can at least be aware of what is going on in the world around you and receive important emergency updates along the way.

<u>***Using a Walkie Talkie***</u>

Walkie Talkies are a great way to stay in contact with a close knit group of people over short distances. And if there is ever an emergency they can be much more effective than using a conventional cell phone. So if you would like to save money on your phone bill you could switch to these classic pieces of communication equipment for the short term in order to keep your dialogue alive!

Chapter 4: Low Budget Medicine and Herbal Healing

When cash is low and an illness strikes, things can get pretty rough. This is why it is very important to be able to know some of the rudiment of first aid for yourself so that you can you can manage your health without busting your budget. Here are a few tips how to do jut that!

Have a Good First Aid Kit

One of the most important things that you could ever have in your house is a First Aid Kit! These kit's should consist of at least a bottle of Tylenol (aspirin), some bandages, a needle, cold packs, hydrogen peroxide, scissors, and tweezers. Having a good needle on hand is very important, just in case someone gets a bad cut and needs to have stitches sewn into their skin. With the right knowledge and the right equipment, there is no reason why you can't sew your own stitches. So have these on hand in case you need to administer your own medical treatment.

Aloe Vera

Aloe Vera gel is taken from the Aloe Vera plant and is quite useful when it comes to being able to heal the skin. This stuff was invaluable for me during my last trip to California. During that trip I was burned so bad that almost considered going to the hospital. But not looking forward to emergency room fees that I knew that my health insurance would not cover, I was grateful when a friend offered me the low budget alternative of Aloe Vera! As soon as I smoothed that substance over my skin, I could feel the cool healing effect instantly.

Epsom Salts

Epson salt is incredibly therapeutic and gives us a great feeling of rejuvenation on our joints and muscles. It works well to alleviate pains and aches of all kinds. If you are having a rough time, just soak your feet in a bucket of Epson salt and you will feel a whole lot better in a matter of just minutes. It will help you feel completely rejuvenated.

Garlic

Using Garlic as something other than a pizza topping can do wonders for your health. As it turns out, Garlic works well as a disinfectant. If you have a cut, or even an large open wound. If you can just place some garlic in the abrasion with and wrap it all up with some bandages you will be able to greatly speed up the healing process. Garlic is also known to have direct benefits on the immune system, helping to boost the body's defenses against dysentery, cholera, typhus, and a few other ailments. So it could do you a world of good just o have some good old garlic in your medicine cabinet!

Wild Violets

A lot of people are not aware of this, but the wild violet flower is not only beautiful to look at, but it is also completely chock full of vitamins that are good for your health! Wild Violets just happen to be full of both Vitamin C and Vitamin A, giving your body a great boost when it needs it, without spending a ton of money on multivitamins!

Consuming roughage such as these can help your health and your wallet! The roots of these plants are also known for their therapeutic properties when it comes to relieving that aches and pains of joints. So if you ever find yourself with a bad ankle just grind up some wild violet root and massage it into your throbbing foot and you will inevitably feel a whole lot better. These are all great ways to use low budget medicine and herbal healing.

Conclusion: The Best Way to Save Money!

In the end the best way that you could ever possibly save money would be to be plan ahead and weight your options. Just by taking the time to think clearly you can save yourself a ton of cash. Money is mostly wasted during quick minute decisions that are not thought through very well. In order to make the best of any situation, we need to use our brain. I hope that this book has opened your mind up to some of the possibilities.

FREE Bonus Reminder

If you have not grabbed it yet, please go ahead and download your special bonus report
"Preppers Survival Guide. Proven Tactics For Armed Incounters!"
Simply Click the Button Below

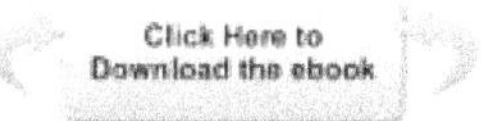

OR **Go to This Page**
http://preppersliving.com/free

BONUS #2: More Free & Discounted Books & Products

Do you want to receive more Free/Discounted Books or Products?
We have a mailing list where we send out our new Books or Products when they go free or with a discount on Amazon. Click on the link below to sign up for Free & Discount Book & Product Promotions.
=> Sign Up for Free & Discount Book & Product Promotions <=

OR Go to this URL
http://zbit.ly/1WBb1Ek